JIM SPARROW OF WOODFORD GREEN

16 — 9 — 007

To Jack
Keep Listening my old Pal
"Jim Sparrow"
might be in your Garden.
With Best Wishes
Percy Salmon
Author

Jim Sparrow of Woodford Green

Essex Tales of Feather & Fur

by

Percy Salmon

Nomlas Press

First published in 2007 by Nomlas Press
147 Pyrles Lane, Loughton
Essex IG10 2NH
www.amolibros.co.uk

Distributed by Gazelle Book Services Limited
Hightown, White Cross Mills, South Rd
Lancaster, England LA1 4XS

British Library Cataloguing in Publication Data
A catalogue record for this book is available from the
British Library.

ISBN 978-0-9540055-2-8

Typeset by Amolibros, Milverton, Somerset
This book production has been managed by Amolibros
Printed and bound by T J International Ltd, Padstow, Cornwall, UK

1

Ambrosia Avenue

Ambrosia Avenue, Woodford Green, without a shadow of doubt, was the very best of one of many similar avenues and drives, which made up this community of tree-lined pavements and pretty well-kept gardens.

No 47 was an old property, now painted white, with original handmade roofing tiles. Chimney stacks or seasonal melody platforms of various sizes protruded in five different places, having witnessed many changes over the years, not only to family names that had come and gone, but also to the Creatures of Daylight and Nocturnal Adventures. They, like the human beings, had experienced changes that had to be accepted, and had had to accept the progress of time, from whatever part of front or rear garden they had made their habitat.

The south-facing rear elevation had enjoyed for many years the company of a magnificent wisteria, from the first bluish-lilac blossoms appearing in late spring and early summer, to the

weaker blooms appearing continuously right through into early autumn. From ground to roof level, it covered the total area en-masse, going round, up and over the extensions built over time. During that period, as you can imagine, many creatures had made use of this spectacular residence, not only a multitude of honey bees, bumble bees, and the like, but also feathered varieties of birds. They made sure of their early claim to this elite palace for building rights each season, an important decision that appeared to be an agreement as soon as the cake had been cut. Then both cock and hen birds appeared to be as one, for many a feathered fight had taken place for the right to build a nest, lay their eggs, hatch their young, and be prepared to survive. With what rewards! A grandstand view twenty-four hours a day of every incident.

Both front and back gardens were designed to high standards, with evergreen trees, leylandii, bay, and holly, and the odd-shaped hawthorn. Pear and apple trees of many years vintage were placed at strategic spots to give excellent positions to the many songsters who even in this day and age tried to assist in a dawn chorus, as youngsters wanted to know what Father was doing when he was not taking his turn at feeding them during nesting time.

Shrubs too, from all parts of the globe were permanently established here, with variegated ivies forming carpets of astonishing patterns. Almost every square yard or metre had a seasonal nest of some description, be it that of mouse, vole, dormouse, or many another four-footed friend or foe. Also many different species of surface runners formed their own pathways, and tunnels like the centipedes, millipedes and May bugs, with of course spiders by the million, and under the ground munching away, hundreds of thousands of worms, destined to be enjoyed by all the spring, summer, autumn, and winter workers. You can just imagine raised walkways overlooking carefully planned beds and borders, cascades of blooming seasonal flowers, and at the lower end a fish pond with its own fountain, each and every one of the inhabitants rejoicing in the many happy times and sympathising with the sorrowful occasions that No 47 householders and lodgers had successively gone through down the ages.

So you may gather that this human community of urban dwellers loved their feathered friends, giving priority to every bird, be they robins, wrens, blue tits, great tits, coal tits, nuthatches, tree

creepers, chaffinches, greenfinches, goldfinches, starlings, blackbirds, song thrushes, mistle thrushes, and providing up-market feeding arrangements for all comers. Even jays, jackdaws and crows made occasional calls to see if there was anything they might be interested in. The magpies were not welcome visitors in many of the gardens, though they together with pigeons made snap appearances at Number 47.

Of course there was always gossip going on at feeding times, when the many food dispensers were topped up – might be any time of the day, winter or summer. It was then that the old sparrow usually muscled in, from his perch higher up the tree, with words of wisdom. These were often remarks directed at any one of the timid birds, who were always a trifle backward when it came to coming forward, and attempting to get their share of what was on offer.

More often than not a bird, perhaps a blue tit, would be unable to use the bird feeders, because he was continually been bullied and bashed about.

The old sparrow would call the bird to one side and give it a few words of advice, telling him…

If you think you are beaten, you are!

If you think you will come second, you will!

Success is all in the mind, if you think they are better than you—they will be!

You have to say to yourself, I am as good as any other bird, and keep repeating this, and, sooner or later, you'll be in there scrapping for yourself and your family. Because you have convinced everyone you can succeed.

Life's battles don't always go to the stronger or faster bird, but sooner or later the bird who wins is the bird who knows he can.

By being positive through challenges and changes you'll be bold and grow!

What a wonderful atmosphere with all this free education for feathered families to get acquainted. Just the job to start on life's ladder being guided by the kindly old philosophy of an intellectual sparrow!

You can quite understand why 47 Ambrosia

Avenue was a property that had a high reputation for being first with all the latest news and information, for those meetings around the bird table were instantly dispatched to all parts of the creature community.

Jim through his lifetime had been Baby Jim, Big Jim and now he was Grandpa Jim. Brothers, uncles, any male sparrow—they would all be known as Jim, but sisters, aunts and any female sparrows were known as Jane right up to Grandma Jane who now was sadly across the garden in another of the bottle trees, which everybody called the SR (Sparrows Rest), her departure there decided when she was unable to hop from one bough to another. She was very happy there, as many of her own age group were residents also, all with old-age problems.

Grandpa Jim was now living in semi-retirement in the lower regions of the Leylandii Bottle (if you imagine a bottle with a long neck upside down) and among his various tasks as the Warden who vetted most of the visiting relations from nearby gardens, was making sure that no sparrow or any intruder could move up from the ground some eight feet down. This residence, which had been in the family for many generations, had seen many changes through the years, and now Grandpa Jim in the twilight of his long life was often to be found chatting away to his many nieces, nephews, grand- and great-grand-sparrows. One of his many assets were the darker brown chest feathers in the shape of a shield, which he regularly liked to prune.

He could recall stories by the barrow-load of how countless intruders of all feathered varieties had not only tried to muscle in but had even tried to become permanent residents The magpies, who were wholesale thieves, had tried aggressively on several occasions to steal, not only eggs and young fledglings, but also parent sparrows who were sitting guarding their nests.

The Leylandii Bottle through the years had gradually matured and now the tree was almost as broad as it was high with the bole as thick as a telephone pole. So you can be sure there were no worries about its strength: all the hundreds of branches which were directly at right angles to the trunk, were perfect for the various floors, where each age group was usually to be found continuously squabbling about rankings. The top was rounded like a gherkin, and had look-out positions – North, South, East, and West. The whole tree, being an evergreen, had a soft feathery leaf and its shape was maintained every autumn by the gardeners of the elderly owners of the property.

The Des Res, as all the family liked to call it, was a property worthy of the neighbourhood, the lower branches used for disobedient and wayward offspring. In fact, a minority would purposely get into trouble and in some sparrows' bad books, just to be down below listening to Grandpa Jim's recollections and stories, and to understand from this wise old bird why misbehaviour was not to be taken lightly, and should be avoided at every reasonable level.

There were also committee rooms about halfway up. Meetings held here would always disturb the neighbourhood with the constant chattering and squawking that went on. The Seniors would persevere with the agenda, when more often than not Grandpa Jim in his role as chairman would finally say, "I am going to hop down and look after my responsibilities on the registration Branch."

So then everyone would go back to their own levels to continue discussing the committee's conclusions, disagreeing or approving, even when the night porter up on the very top bough had made it quite clear that it was now time to perch up and pack up.

Today there had been a longer meeting than usual, and Grandpa Jim had already made

arrangements to have a chat with his pal Nutty the squirrel. Of course he had to tell him when he arrived on his bough, why there had been such a strong debate that had lasted so long.

Of course Nutty wanted to know why such a fierce argument had been taking place, for as he said, "Most of neighbourhood's Feathered Friend Society (FFS) were quite anxious to know what on earth was going on in the Des Res."

More often than not, like today, Grandpa Jim told him, it was a young upstart, a last year's novice, who had taken up with a female, and wanted to move in on the eighth floor to start building a nest in preparation for next spring.

He had tried to get through to Bird Brain as he liked to call this season's youngster, that it was only early November and there was plenty of time, so he made a definite proposal, which had a majority approval, that they both get together and give that part of the floor, which earlier in the spring and summer had comprised as many as six nests, a good old tidy-up. They should also make sure that the position they selected for their nest was not directly under the ninth-floor nests. He tried hard to impress on them that this was most important, because the pooh droppings from the floors above had caused many problems in the Des Res through the years.

Nutty was a wise old squirrel, and proved this point by saying, "Most of the younger ones, I find, are all tarred with the same brush. You don't seem to be able to tell them anything, because they know it all. Our youngsters have been told time and time again not to get involved outside the neighbourhood, whether it's thieving other squirrels' left-outs or robbing birds' feeding boxes. It stands to reason that Greytop the Gangster squirrel will get his revenge sometime, when an opportunity arises."

They continued chatting away to each other, telling various tales about where they had brought up their many families through their lifetime.

Nutty managed to repeat a couple of his stories, and Grandpa Jim told him, "I know what's the matter with you, it's your memory, and old age. It's like mine at times."

Straightaway Nutty said, "It's true, do you know I cannot remember where I have buried my conkers and acorns that I've collected round the Cricket Field, and that was only a couple of weeks ago. Oh! And my peanuts."

Grandpa Jim said, "I nearly got banished into

the Sparrow Cell, only last week, when I nearly let in, here in the Registration Department, one of the squatters from off the Common and you know what they are like. It was a good job that my eldest grandson had followed him in and asked him what floor he was living on. Of course this confused him, and without further questioning he just flew straight down and away. You must have heard the din, because all the fifth and seventh floors flew out and chased him almost to the start of the Common."

Finishing their chat, Grandpa Jim said, "I think we have got to accept this, Nutty, our brains are just like the Long Legs (human ones). As we get older our brains are not so active, for when you think how much wear they've had, it's marvellous how they cope… . I can hear some trouble up top again, see you sometime."

He hopped up between the branches, thinking to himself how quick he used to be when the races were held. They used to start at the top of the Tree, just two sparrows: fly down to the ground, through the branches, pick up a matchstick then back to the top Committee Room, where six Judges presided. They would verify with the circuit Marshals that no cheating (i.e. short cuts or bribes) had taken place. Then the Champion for the Week was proclaimed, and Grandpa Jim liked to recount that he had once held the title for three weeks one summer. And the Marathons!

They were four circuits round the Leylandii with both sparrows flying in opposite directions – what memories he had! Mind you, he still played an important part in that race, for each bird had to pass through his Basement Branch, where this was recorded by Grandpa Jim's No 2. This was normally a sparrow who had misbehaved, and was two branches lower than Grandpa Jim's Basement Branch and not so far off the ground. The punishment here was that you had to stay awake for twenty-four hours. Then of course all the Night Prowlers were on the move after darkness had set in. This brought out Sniffy the Tabby Cat (so called as he had nasal problems), so all naughty sparrows had to be on high alert during their time on the Sin Bin Branch.

It was strange that his last thought was about Sniffy, for on arrival Jim Sparrow No 9 in the pecking order was waiting with a question for him, asking him straightaway about the problems that Sniffy the Tabby Cat was causing not only to all the birdlife in the garden, but also to neighbouring ones as well.

"Do you mind if I get my breath back first? I find it a struggle to get up to these meetings now. It wouldn't be so bad if these meetings were called only once a day, but lately it's every few hours, maybe four times a day."

There then came a response which made him feel proud to be the Big Chief, for all the eight members said in unison, "You take your time, Grandpa Jim, for we're just pleased that you're still able to make these meetings at your age."

Reminding himself of Sniffy the Tabby Cat, and the anxiety that creature had caused, he realised how important this meeting was going to be as he looked down and around at his fellow committee members. On a branch just above them, as usual, most of this year's hatchlings were sitting around ready for the wise words that Grandpa Jim would offer, but they could all see how the flight up had made him out of breath and sapped his energy.

As usual, though, within a couple of minutes he was back to normal, making sure that the points he wanted to emphasise were quite clear. After being told that Sniffy had claimed another one of this season's youngsters, it was obvious to him that drastic action would now have to be taken. That wicked cat had taken a total of four sparrows and that just would not do.

By this time the meeting of the senior members had been joined by all the other sparrows in the Leylandii, all trying to butt in with ideas and suggestions, keen to earn plaudits and impress Grandpa Jim with their intelligence.

In fact Grandpa Jim was quite impressed with one of last year's hatchlings more modern thinkers. He would on his reckoning be No 14 and was saying, "We ought to drive him out of our garden for good, then he could upset birds in other people's gardens." No 14 then went on to propose that the Six Aerial Bombers, of which he was a proud member, get practising straightaway if the plan he'd put forward was to be agreed. There was quite a noisy discussion about this, and near neighbours must have thought there'd been a calamity of some sort by the racket which was going on inside the Leylandii. But strategy was vital: times, positions and would have to be carefully checked and dummy runs monitored to make sure that accuracy and timing were spot on.

Grandpa Jim finally closed the meeting by saying, "I'll leave it with you all – the plan's to be put into operation just as Sniffy comes out a little before dusk tomorrow evening."

How lucky he reckoned, going back down to his branch, that the Jim Sparrow in charge of the Leylandii Sun Dial had been present at the meeting. What a godsend the flagpole had been when it had been installed, for now its shadow, which formed all round the Des Res, was telling correct times all through the day. So Dropping Hour, or D Hour as they called it, was to be thirty hours away.

Unbeknown to Grandpa Jim, about half a dozen or more of this season's youngsters had overheard that there was going to be an aerial bombardment of Sniffy and had decided to try out and experiment this dive-bombing performance about three branches up, but away from where Grandpa Jim was having a late siesta. They were using the actual branch which was going to be the main assault branch for take off, so you can gather there was an enormous amount of chattering going on, there being only just enough room for one sparrow to go through the hole at a time – a tiny hole worn away over time through the outside leaves of the Leylandii. Three sparrow nearby had appointed themselves stewards, to make sure the exercise was reasonably marshalled. All three were Sniffers (so called because they was sucking the resin from the Leylandii) who had tried to bring their bad habits to the Des Res, thankfully without success, since their parents had been wiped out by a virus a few years ago. It was a case of each trying to get out of the hole first, so there was a lot of pushing and shoving, as each sparrow became more and more excited as they made their flights.

Then the inevitable occurred! Four trying to get out through the hole at once tumbled towards the ground before they had time to open their wings, and then, oh dear. The very next thing there was a flash of Sniffy and the tabby cat leapt upwards and grabbed two before they had a chance to take flight. Then there was a storm of feathers floating to the ground as both sparrows were very quickly dispatched

by Sniffy and then disposed of under the wheelbarrow.

You can imagine all the bird population, not only in this garden, but also all the neighbouring ones, making enough noise to make you think that Christmas might have come early, or another magpie had passed on. But very soon those noisy voices changed their tune after hearing that Sniffy the tabby had added two more sparrows to his growing list of scalped sparrows.

Grandpa Jim had witnessed only part of what had happened when Sniffy the Tabby had withdrawn under the wheelbarrow, so he could not verify how long the wretch had been hiding away before he had pounced on the hapless youngsters. Certainly he must have crept in there when the meeting was being held earlier in the afternoon, and this is exactly what he told the committee meeting, instantly called within a few minutes of the disaster. It appeared that both the sparrows who were the latest victims of Sniffy the tabby had been involved with the Sniffers. That awful habit made them do silly things which they did not realise were doing them harm and they weren't responsible for their behaviour.

It was agreed after much discussion that, as things stood, this should be the No 1 subject at the next weekly meeting. Right now the urgent business was to move the D Hour forward by several hours, for it was a sure thing that when

Sniffy came out for his catnap just after noon tomorrow, there must not be any mistakes, and most importantly, that no more lives were to be lost.

Grandpa Jim again spoke about the worry that this season's youngsters were causing their family residence. In fact he had noticed some who were wearing part of their feathers on top like the old

Red Indians he had been told about, all spiky in appearance. This was soon shouted down, even bright-thinking Jim Sparrow No 14 said, "Grandpa Jim, you have got to move with the times."

There was now another hold-up. Just as Grandpa Jim was thinking it's time to stop talking and let the practice get underway, a starling messenger dropped by to say that the murmuration of starlings that were gathering to fly out of the country was parking up in the hornbeam tree for a few nights, and wanted to know if help was required to unload some more material on Sniffy. If so, then please to tell the messenger what time they were needed.

"What wonderful news!" Grandpa Jim exclaimed. "We would only need a couple of dozen from their Squelchy Squadron to put on a sparkling performance." Straightaway the starling messenger was informed of the times they would like their volunteers to arrive, approximately three minutes past D hour. It would be the duty and privilege of all the sparrows attached to the Dive Bombers unit to have the first shot at Sniffy. And by the noise that was going on from another part of the garden, the Sparrow Dive Bombers was getting mighty efficient and close to the dummy targets.

The voting was unanimous at the Extraordinary Meeting, so as dusk, then nightfall finally arrived, the garden and neighbourhood gradually settled down again to await events tomorrow.

By daybreak every winged variety had been informed of the plot to disorganise and disorientate Sniffy. The senior cook had been busy long before sunrise plotting what she could conjure up for the squashiest despatches and smelliest odours, for this toxic midday special had to be taken in at one end and delivered from the other within a few seconds.

In fact by the time D hour minus one had arrived, the old pigeon nest was half filled with the most noxious material, this now being the loading bay for the Sparrow Squadron.

In fact, so confident was the sparrow in charge of Operations, that he had given permission for two of the worst Sniffers to take part, after they'd said they were sorry that they had got involved with the glue from the tree.

Word had gone up to headquarters from Wally the Wren that Sniffy had been seen sneaking through the ivy-covered old herbaceous border (which gave him lots of cover so most could not spot him), obviously already waiting for another victim. There was only the one way in and out, and if the early marksmen were successful and made some direct hits, as had been planned, when he came out he'd have to go across the wide expanse of lawn to escape.

Everything went like clockwork, for the crack down the boards on the wheelbarrow had been made wider by a couple of inches in the night by ten field mice who were keen not to be left out of Operation "Sniffy". It was an oak-boarded one, and one mouse who had been doing hard labour for pinching grain from

another Mickey Mouse's Winter Harvest Store had worked all through the night helping with this, thereby earning several days' remission on his punishment. Word also came through that his teeth had been worn in places to his gums!

The drop was dead on time after the church clock on the green struck its first peal at noon. Then for the next five minutes there was utter bedlam as each succeeding dive was so accurate, on the part of the Sparrow Dive Bombers that Grandpa Jim in his grandstand seat counted hits every single time down the boards of the wheelbarrow.

The Squadron had really done the business for their pooh-dropping assault had penetrated the wheelbarrow and Sniffy had decided to stick his head out to find out what on earth was going on. Not realising that he was the target of this aerial assault he soon went back under the wheelbarrow to decide what action to take.

It was too late, for the Starling Squelchies had arrived and were dropping pooh in huge dollops. This was too much for Sniffy so he decided to make a run for it. By now, he was not sure which way was the right way to get away from this horrible, evil-smelling, nauseating, disgusting stink that had not only almost blinded him but had covered nearly every part of the fur coat that he was so proud of. He had lost all sense of direction for there was no let-up – the Sparrow Squadron

had reloaded and were now sending down more vile pooh. The effect was extra strong, for as the Sparrow Cook had said, these droppings were designed for rapid release. Rhubarb leaves had been part of her recipe and included towards the bottom of the pigeon's nest. As most good gardeners know, when it starts to ferment and rot, that is where the goodness lies.

Sniffy, by this time, had managed to get away from most of the dive-bombers' action and had disappeared into the garden next door, where there was more cover for him.

Grandpa Jim, using the peals of the church bells at one o'clock as a signal, had called a meeting up in the committee room and right away he began by saying, "Without a doubt this had been one of my most enjoyable days whilst living here in the Des Res, but we must not forget our poor young sparrows who have given their lives. Without their loss, this triumphant operation would never have taken place. Our revenge has been ably administered and was fully justified. I am sure," he continued, "that this was a wonderful combined effort. What surprises me is that in similar circumstances in the past, we had not thought to hand out this sort of treatment. I feel sure that Sniffy will not be worrying any of the birdlife in this and neighbouring gardens for a very long time. Before I close what I would like us all to think about now is how we can deal with the magpies and the rats—and, worst of all, the pigeons, wood and feral, all of them thieves, rogues and vagabonds."

The Wise old Owl, who had been watching most of the entertainment from his roost way up in the oak tree, continued his observations and it was not until early evening that he sent a message to Grandpa Jim to say that it was an operation that had been long overdue. He concluded that success is not measured by how you do compared to how somebody else has done. Success is measured by how you do compared to what you could have done with what you have inherited.

Sniffy ventured out from under the rose bushes just before the garden lights came on and then ran for his life away from the fish pond where the lights had reflected the terrible state of his fur. Still unable to see clearly, he did the wisest thing and crept away to hide from all those unseen pairs of eyes who were tracking his every move.

2

STORYTIME

It was also, now that the winter months were fast approaching, the time that Grandpa Jim would relate stories to younger generations and sometimes as many as fifteen Sparrows would sit round. These talks would take place on a Thursday afternoon and now and again a remark made by Grandpa Jim would start off a debating issue. He quite enjoyed this, for he not only answered the many questions put to him, but it also made the time go quickly. This particular story, he had told so many times down through the years, repeated again and again from the distant past, that he almost knew it off by heart,

and also wished that those good old days would come back again – that's how some feathered friends considered the good old days.

The church clock on the Green clanged twice, and already a large gathering of all age groups had gathered in the Committee Room, awaiting Grandpa's Jim arrival. Before he began, he had several beakfuls of his favourite tipple from his own half-coconut shell. (This again had seen some wear and tear down through time: Chairman's Privilege!)

“The story I am going to tell you this afternoon took place at a time,” he began, “when flocks of sparrows were not only classed as one of Man’s best friends, but also one of Man’s worst enemies!”

There was quite a lot of “Oohs” and “Aahs” and “can’t be’s” from all around the branches. After this brief commotion had quietened down, Grandpa Jim continued, “Yes, that’s correct. And now we must press on, for this genuine Sparrow Story took place fifty years ago. About that time some of the farmers around the district held a meeting concerning the mischief that the Sparrow was doing to the farmers in general and in particular to the cereal crops being grown. One farmer had put forward figures that from his own observation, he was losing a bushel per acre, or in other words three million bushels a year, or in money £700.000. He himself killed as many sparrows as he could and in some of their criminal little stomachs he had found as many as eight to twelve grains of corn.”

Now this caused lots of noise from all quarters, for most of those who had not heard the story before, could not believe there was so much injustice done to the Jim Sparrows of long ago. Grandpa Jim fluttered his wings resignedly: "If you want me to finish the story, I don't want to have any more interruptions. What we have to remember is the Sparrow eats no end of insects, that destroy scores of thousands of stalks of corn when young. Therefore if a sparrow eats between the months of September to July perhaps only a hundred of these insects, he might with a good deal of honesty say that he has a right to a small share of the grain which he has preserved.

"However, a sparrow at the time, who was a clever, quite knowledgeable chap, heard about this by way of Travelling Sparrow tales and it so appeared that the farm where he had made his home was the one where the very same farmer had been boasting of killing as many of the sparrows as he could, and then searching their poor little stomachs to find out how many grains of corn they had been tucking away.

One particular day the sparrow was out during the early morning searching for grubs and insects for his growing family in one of the farmer's barns. While he was foraging, he came across the farmer, and told him in no uncertain terms what he thought of him and the reasons why he felt that there had been a total injustice done to him and

all his fellow comrades. "For eight months of the year I have nothing but insects to eat, and you can see me any day you like, hopping about in the fields looking for them. During the other four months I manage to pick up a good deal of grain, and some fruit, but if I had stayed away from the farm for the whole twelve months, the insects would have eaten many times more grain and fruit than I could ever manage to get. So that is why, as a matter of fact, I think myself entitled to a portion of grain when it is ripening. If it had not been for me there would not have been so many ears of grain as there are. Nor do I think it fair that you should go and examine our stomachs for grain during harvest time, unless you're going to do the same thing to insects at other times of the year. We work hard for our grain, and you never seem to think of that! It is only when the fields are getting ready for the harvest and the reaper that farmers like you, think of us as a pest.

"In winter, it is true, we do try to get some of the food that's thrown out for the chickens, pigeons and all our other feathered friends; after all, we must live somehow, and when the ground is frozen hard, what are we to do? Starve and eat nothing? Nobody talks about exterminating us or telling the world how many grains of corn we have in our greedy criminal stomachs then! Or write to newspapers about us being a nuisance. No, it's never until Harvest Time!

"Nobody sees us toiling away for our food at other times, but as soon as it's time to gather in the crops, the old fuss and bother about us starts all over again. For I don't mind telling you, Mr Farmer, we all look upon the end of August as a kind of Little Birds' Carnival. When we do live it up! Admittedly we collect in flocks and go and eat our fill if we can in the cornfields. You farmers can see us move in. Yes, we fly about in our hundreds; we settle down and there's chattering and laughing. What goes on is exactly what goes on at one of your Farmers Wives' Meetings. But out in the cornfields it's different – somebody calls out, 'The sparrow club is here,' and then shoot us down by the score, count the grains in our stomachs, and tell the world how many there were."

There was a very respectable silence after Grandpa Jim had emphasized his final words, and the silence continued until he told them, "It's worth reminding you all about this farmer and why, now and again, we will meet up with the likes of him, even nowadays. Just think of what he did, examining our criminal little stomachs like that! If he had done this when there was no grain in the cornfields, our little tummies would have been found to contain several different insects, and that, taking the one against the other – a grain of corn against an insect – the sparrow would have been found in the long run to have put more corn into the barns than he kept out of it!"

Finishing the story, Grandpa Jim told them, "The Smart Sparrow flew off his perch on the top of the walking stick that the farmer had driven into the ground, leaving the farmer scratching his head in disbelief, and no doubt wondering whether there really was any truth in the sparrow's argument, which he had to admit to himself he had not even considered. How astonished the farmer was at being ticked off like this! He did not like it one little bit, and during this whole lecture had not said one word. Opening and closing his mouth, no words came out at all; he was speechless!"

Grandpa Jim was then inundated with questions from all the various age groups. Those who had heard this story before still fired questions just like the ones who were hearing this tale for the first time – their thirst for knowledge quickly quenched.

"Why don't we see flocks of sparrows now?"

"How many sparrows would there have been in a flock?"

"Were there many cornfields, if so were there any near here in those days?"

"Do you think, Grandpa Jim, that, as we take grains of corn from the bird boxes and bird tables, we've got criminal little stomachs?"

"Who was the Smart Sparrow, and are we related to him?"

Grandpa Jim answered this one very thoughtfully but rather cagily, saying, "Yes of course we all are."

Really, he knew that his dad was the Smart Sparrow and that every few years he was reborn, with all the knowledge, intelligence, of thousands of lifetimes. He knew too that it would not be long before such a rebirth was going to be the order of a new breeding season. He had seen a lot of seasons come and go, and was now certainly in the twilight years of his life.

How did he know this?

It was his duty at nesting time to go round to the various nests, maybe sixteen or so, and inspect their clutches of four to six greyish-coloured eggs, dashed with mottles of brown. In most cases just one egg might be different from the others, a much lighter one in colour all over, but the important egg which concerned him was the one which did not have any mottles of brown at all! There would be just the one big blotch of deep brown and this was in the nest chosen to hold another baby miracle for future generations.

It was now time to close up shop, so Grandpa Jim told them, "The Smart Sparrow went on to fight many battles for us all and will continue to do so. Some humans are never grateful when anyone does them a kindness. This happens every day of every week and I want you all to remember this."

3

Wayward Offspring

One afternoon, when the district's 'Spy in the Sky', Spotter the Skylark, plus some of the larger patrol birds had forecast that it would rain continuously for several hours, Grandpa Jim invited members of the FFS to come along to the committee room, to discuss some business that he considered to be of some urgency; in fact, he had been carefully planning for just such a day for some time!

Word quickly went round to the senior Members, and by the time the church clock had completed its two peals, some fifteen pairs of various representatives of the local feathered fraternity had gathered to hear what Grandpa Jim had to say, for every parent bird knew at once why he had called this bird-talk discussion.

Each parent knew that their offspring were causing the neighbourhood untold misery, with their waywardness, rudeness, and downright irresponsible behaviour, not only to the older generations of the FFS but also to the Long Legs, the providers of a big percentage of everyday food provisions.

Charles Chaffinch, sitting next to George and Georgina Tree Sparrow, whispered to them, "Crafty old devil! We suspected it wouldn't be long before he decided that enough is enough and it's not before time that our youngsters are going to have to accept what's coming to them. We have said several times there's going to be trouble ahead, if they don't change their ways! But when we tell our growing family how they should be decent, genuine and honest members of the neighbourhood they don't seem to want to listen. All they say to us is, 'We are bored, there is nothing to do.' "

All the parent birds, now looking round at each other, had realised Grandpa Jim had called in both parents of the worst offenders and most parents noticed that Jim's own grandsons' parents, three of his many sons with their spouses, were also present. One of those happened to be dad to one of the Sniffers, who was also one of the leading trouble-makers according to the whispers that were now circulating as the volume of chit-chat grew louder and louder.

"Quiet please." Grandpa Jim's voice always had an authoritative tone, which instantly calmed the noise down, and demanded attention. So this quickly did the trick, for now a very serious hush had moved along each branch, and every beak and claw was now facing towards Grandpa Jim. He quickly looked round, and noted that Thomas and Tilly Great Tit were not in attendance. He knew the reason—they must be embarrassed about coming along, for they were both pillars of strength in the FFS.

Every parent knew that their eldest girl—Trudie—was very much involved with youthful misdemeanours and unbirdlike behaviour, and had been getting familiar with groups from outside. She was causing her parents enormous worry.

Grandpa Jim called over one of the two stewards who were on duty and spoke to him in a very demanding voice, which made even the boldest parents present take notice and say under their breath, "He certainly means business this afternoon." He told the steward that he wanted Thomas and Tilly to stop whatever they were doing and come along at once, for when he asked them to attend, he expected them to be here with all the other parents, who were now waiting for the meeting to start. It seemed only a few minutes had passed when they arrived via the Exit Branch, squeezed themselves between their other relatives and were now ruffling their feathers and preening themselves. Thomas mumbled a few words of apology, and the meeting was ready to start.

With a nod of his head, Grandpa Jim, with a small cane, which on these occasions seemed to be a permanent fixture in his bill (known to older members of the FFS as the Beaver Bill, this small object could tell many stories of its strength and durability), tapped it on the empty upturned shell of the coconut hanging from the branch

immediately above his head. The resulting 'Bong' let everyone present know the meeting was now getting underway.

As was usual, Grandpa Jim thanked everyone for coming along on an afternoon that might have been more happily spent, and with his normal aplomb, got straight into why it was important to deal with the behaviour of some of the youngsters—all the parents must realise that their offspring were now not only trying to terrorise the feathered fraternity of the neighbourhood, but also feathered kind's considerate benefactors, the Long Legs! With this remark, he held up one wing: "Yes, I know my own kith and kin are demonstrating this dreadful behaviour too, and that is why all of us present must try to find a solution to this ongoing problem." Instantly the chattering became more subdued.

Grandpa Jim continued by telling them about The Smart Sparrow who had experienced the same sort of situations earlier on in the last century, after both the World Wars: "It was a time when there was much discontent with Long Legs, and animals and birds of all sizes and stations in life were trying to rebuild broken homes, broken

lives, and even broken communities. It affected not only their own young Long Legs, but also our own young fledglings, everyone finding it difficult to accept that discipline and consideration to others had to be made permanent for all future generations.

"Yes, The Smart Sparrow helped to re-establish not only the bird neighbourhood, which I might add was many, many times stronger in population. As I mentioned a while ago, there were flocks of sparrows with as many as several hundred in them. So when one was misbehaving, there was as many as fifty others wanting a part of the action, and that was only the sparrow contingent. Perhaps there was a score or more tree sparrows—they always appeared to be more upper-class than us but that didn't make any difference because they had problem youngsters as well. The Smart Sparrow had ideas and answers that proved themselves right at the time."

Grandpa Jim, now realising that he had nearly one hundred per cent of the attending parents listening to his powerful recollections of the Smart Sparrow, continued, telling them that ways and means could be found to cure the sickness that the young birds had brought on themselves. Yes, he felt sure this was only a temporary blip in their education but before he suggested what remedies The Smart Sparrow would have undertaken, he wanted to hear what ideas parents had to try to

resolve the daily headaches that were with them all as each new dawn approached.

This, as you can gather really set the cat amongst the pigeons, for each and every one had firm views as to how to deal with their wayward offspring. Stan Starling and his good lady Samantha, the largest couple here this afternoon, along with Grandpa Jim, were very much involved in helping to resolve the present predicament, having being part of the community for several years. Though most of their family had flown the roost, it was his younger brother's Spindle's youngsters, Steph, Sheila, and Sophie who, by all accounts, appeared to be three of the ring-leaders,

doing some very unladylike things. Stan was trying to get himself heard and was finally allowed to start his speech, after Grandpa Jim had whacked the coconut gong several times to try to get some order.

Stan immediately apologized, adding, "I know that our youngsters are causing lots of trouble in the neighbourhood, but how they have got tangled up with this sort of behaviour neither Sam or myself can understand." This instantly got a reaction from Goldie and Gladys the goldfinch couple, when they both said in unison, "We have seen with our own eyes your brothers' three girls and the blackbird boys Spick, Span, and Sparkle, diving and swooping down, poohing on Number 55's clothes line when Long Legs sheets and linens have been put out to dry and generally causing a disturbance to all at 55. They are a dear old-aged Long Legs who keep the bird tables stocked with all sorts of goodies for us—in summer and winter."

Grandpa Jim now broke in to ask, "Well Stan, what sort of suggestions do you have to help get rid of the troublemakers?" Holding up one of his wings he added, "I know as you all disapprove of the word troublemakers, I have a very suitable name, which I am sure you will accept, it's quick and easy, I call them the four Bs."

From across the all branches came the cry, "What does that stand for?"

Grandpa Jim was highly delighted to the response he gave, when he said, "It stands for the BOROUGH'S BIRD BRAIN BRAWLERS."

Each and every bird present fluttered their wings and signified their approval, and even Grumbler the Greenfinch, who had recently lost Jemima, his wife of many years, nodded and did a little jig on his piece of branch. Grandpa Jim said, "In the Long Legs world, as we all know, they are named and shamed, and they are called ASBO! The O added is an ORDER for discipline in the community to be complied to."

Stan Starling freely admitted he did not like the limelight, but at meetings was always keen to express his philosophy to those whom he knew were good listeners: but today he really took off, for what incensed him more than anything was the fact that his own nieces were deeply implicated in the neighbourhood's problems.

"First of all," he said, "I would like to see the parents convey to their offspring as soon as they are born the importance of behaving themselves and listening to what their parents have to say. They should be told not to take any notice of nearby nests and the obedience problems going on in them, because I feel sure that other fledglings are having an enormous affect on young Spindle's girls..." He was unable to complete this sentence, because half a dozen male birds of different species began to voice their own opinions to him on how to rear their children, each voice overriding the other, as each tried to make himself heard above the rest. This behaviour met with very little approval from Grandpa Jim, who banged the coconut, and the resounding 'Bong' brought order back to the assembly.

Stan Starling continued by telling them he had not come to this meeting to be offensive to any parents; this was how he saw it, and was sure that lessons could be learned directly they had left the egg. He also felt that after they were on the wing, within a few weeks of cracking the shell, this was the time when parent birds should be more involved with them, and not let them have their Flight of Freedom passes so quickly. If they had misbehaved, those passes should *not* be awarded. This last comment immediately met with approval, most parents standing up and stamping their claws on the branches.

Stan continued, on a nod from Grandpa Jim, "I would also suggest that if the situation does not improve, we should all recommend that a conducted visit to the Trauma Tree with Grandpa Jim must be the outcome for a few of our wayward offspring, and this is going to be a difficult choice. Who's to go? This is up to each parent's conscience! Each should say with conviction that one of their youngsters must be one of the young

birds and they are confident that this sort of humiliation will perhaps help us all."

It was time for Grandpa Jim to make his move, for the meeting had now been softened up to expect what he knew was going to be the outcome, and this was just what he had envisaged. Knowing that the Trauma Tree had resolved so many situations in the past that were just like the present one, was it going to scare the youngsters into becoming less boisterous? Grandpa Jim said, "As you parents all seem to be of one mind, so it is now up to us to carry out the wishes of all of us present. Yes, I am quite prepared to take them, no more than eight youngsters, I would suggest. Certainly this outcome would have been the wish of the Smart Sparrow."

He then addressed all those now very interested parents, "You must decide among yourselves which offspring you think will benefit from the visit to the Trauma Tree. I don't want you to think that the suggestion is that we just visit the Tree, that is not an option. I have considered this very carefully and those who you decide are the misfits must stay for at least forty-eight hours. As we all know, the shorter days are already with us, even shorter next week; the daylight hours will be very limited, so we can assume that time spent in the Tree will be very largely in darkness. Now Stan, kindly make some notes as to the ones you think will gain from spending time in the Tree."

While Stan the Starling worked on the choice of delinquent youngsters, with other parents, Grandpa Jim was busy thinking about the Trauma Tree, what it stood for, its stature and the help it had given the community through so many years which might well run into hundreds. The Smart Sparrow had used it many times, and now Grandpa Jim, with his powerful memory, could tell stories, remember incidents, often connected to the weather conditions, and then, like this present crisis, see how the Tree might be a blessing in disguise to everyone. Perhaps this would help young birds get back onto an honest flight path and again be worthy of the FFS.

It was a landmark deciduous tree, because it had very few leaves, those that there were weren't any larger than the common daisy and were shaped like the teaspoons that the Long Legs used.

Mauve bean-like blossoms of the same size appeared in late spring, and tiny bean-shaped seed pods formed through the summer. Where it was depleted of leaves, it made up for with thorns, which covered every twig, branch, bough and trunk; it was the density of those thorns, some as long as seven centimetres, which made it into one of the most formidable trees for miles around. Its position on the Green gave out a silent message loud and clear, "Keep Clear," and every bird flying was warned to avoid the Trauma Tree, while parents earnestly warned their offspring, especially the most wayward.

Oh yes, it had its usual crop of assorted aphids, and as Grandpa Jim always reminded most of the local birds, these creatures formed a letter T right down and across the Trauma Tree. There were thousands of aphids, but the difficulty was how to get to them.

A pair of sparrow hawks, Scud and Speedy, had been associated with this tree from time immemorial, for they had established a nest high up in one of the two lime trees on the church side of the Green, which had been passed down through the family, as their history tells it, the nest first being built when the seedling Trauma Tree arrived on the Green. For many generations there had been a close liaison between Scud, Speedy and the local garden bird communities, so that at certain times of the day they had the privilege of flying round and across without any danger to themselves or kindred. Any birds from outside, not knowing of these arrangements flew in this area at their peril, for if they made a landing in the Trauma Tree… . And here Grandpa Jim usually gave a big sigh, saying nothing more and looking towards the top of the Leylandii. Everyone listening would chill, knowing what might happen to them, but Grandpa Jim said sometimes a happy ending did occur, for sometimes flocks of birds crossed, giving an opportunity for escape by joining them.

As he recognised now from the chatter of the parent birds, the discussion was about the feeding of the youngsters, a major worry for any parent, whatever the species. He could hear the grinding chatter of the greenfinch pair, George's twin brother Grumbler and the female he had recently taken up with, Gill, who had been acting as a foster mum for the five youngsters, but fortunately so far only two were showing signs of disobedience, Gerald and Geoff.

Grandpa Jim knew that he must get the meeting back to reasonable order so gave a good whack on the coconut gong with his cane, and as if by magic there was instant silence, all eyes and ears turned to him. Keeping their young fed whilst they were serving bird time in the Trauma Tree was a subject their chairman was about to address.

Grandpa Jim said, "I know what concerns you

all—while they serve their forty-eight hours—the food situation. Well, I have some good news for you all! I have been making inquiries at No 59, who as we all know are plagued with moles, and according to what I've been told, the Trauma Tree is one of their detention centres too. I have been talking to Muffler the king mole and he tells me he will be highly delighted for two young moles to come and stay for whatever length of time you need them. In fact he will be very grateful if they can come and be good citizens for a short time! At No 59, they had worried the elderly Long Legs since the early part of the summer with their continual hunt for food in all parts of the garden. And the precious lawn in front of the Long Legs' kitchen window is now looking as if a gardener had never been employed for three days every week. Yes, take them off his hands, and we would be doing the mole fraternity a big favour."

There now seemed to be a lot of confusion amongst the parents, for as most of them knew, mole hills were a good source of food for grubs of all length and size, when the moles were tunnelling—disturbing the earth continually, pushing it upwards so that the choice goodies could be quickly grabbed by beaks, bills, claws, or talons. Grandpa Jim spotted this concern, for he continued, "What every one of you doesn't know about the moles is that they work in four-hour intervals around the clock. And this is why I think it is good news for us all, for as there are going to be eight youngsters going to the Trauma Tree, every four hours from daybreak, four birds will drop down, and take what's on offer. Then when the moles cease burrowing, they fly back to their bird cell perch, and wait until it's their turn again. Now any more questions before those you have nominated are sent off to be seen by the medical board, to make sure they will be strong enough to stay and do their bird time in the Trauma Tree?"

There was only the one question put forward by Stan Starling after he had produced his offenders' list, and that was, "Who is on duty most of the time?"

Every parent present knew that Grandpa Jim would shoulder most of the bird warden's duties, so he was quick to answer, "Of course it's going to be no problem, for as you all are aware during daylight hours I shall be in the tree on the observation branch—and don't worry about me, because I shall be flying up and down with each batch of four as they fly down for meal breaks. So I'll be with them, enjoying whatever the moles are providing. As you all know by now two nights are going to be spent in the Trauma Tree, and during that time I have arranged with the Wise Old Owl, for his grandson Trencher, a travelling Tawny, to swoop round the Trauma Tree every half an hour, and give a couple of too-whits as he passes the branch which they all should be sharing. We are in luck because there is a full moon on both nights, so they should see his shape go passing by. He is coming up from the country, and is known in that locality as Trencher the Thinking Tawny, for he has passed five Grade Bird Levels, and hopefully is taking up Community Business Studies, so that he can come round giving advice to boroughs like ourselves, helping us to overcome situations that we all find ourselves in today. This knowledge has been passed to me this very day by Jaws the Jackdaw."

All the parent birds approved this by vibrating each twig and branch with beak, wing, and claw. What was very noticeable now was the fact that the parents' meeting had now doubled in size, and it appeared that every one of the wayward youngsters whom Stan Starling had short-listed were now present, though not necessarily sitting with their own kith and kin. It just shows how word can get around from beak to beak!

Grandpa Jim, seeing they were all there, said, "I can see that we have with us now the youngsters who have been misbehaving. All your mums and dads have agreed that you spend some time in what we all know as the Trauma Tree, and that all of you who have been annoying the neighbourhood will now have to take some of your own medicine. As you know, when us parents have meetings like this, our word is final. My good friend Stan Starling will read out the names and each young bird can ask one question, so go ahead, Stan."

Stan started off by confirming that it would be at tomorrow afternoon's church peal of three o'clock when the youngsters would have to start their bird time. First on his list were his brother's two girls, Steph and Sophie, to which Sophie, the younger of the three girls by five minutes, asked, "We have heard about the few thorns which are in the Trauma Tree. How do you expect us to hop about keeping ourselves amused for all that time?"

Grandpa Jim said, "That's just it, you don't move about. You will be able to hop over each other to keep your mind and body alert and, as I have said before, the opportunity will arise every eight hours for you to fly down off the branch and feed on the grubs which the moles hopefully will be turning out from their tunnel workings. So you can all do your keep-fit wing demonstration displays, but, only under the spread of the Trauma Tree. I would like to emphasise here that the idea of the exercise is to make you all feel very guilty about what you all have been doing to your parents and the neighbourhood in general. As you are making a visit for the first time, you should know that very little of the Trauma Tree internal thorn system is negotiable for anyone to move comfortably about. Remember that any youngster thinking about escaping will have no chance of crossing the Common in any direction, in daylight or darkness, for they will not be returning to the neighbourhood if they try this."

All beaks, eyes, and wings pointed in the direction of Sophie, who was looking very downcast as Stan Starling continued with his list of selected youngsters. "Spick, Span and Sparkle, the blackbird boys. Trudie the daughter of my good friends, Thomas and Tilly Great Tit, and their cousins Billy and Belle Blue Tit's daughter, Bobbie, and last of the eight selected is going to be Charles Chaffinch's one and only daughter Charlotte, nicknamed Char." When this final name was announced, all heads were turned and focused on Charles Chaffinch, for Char was the only culprit not present and there was now complete silence along and over every branch, waiting for a reaction from the old Chap himself.

Grandpa Jim noticed his discomfort, and quietly said to him, "Now Charles, have you any reason as to why Char should not join the other seven Youngsters in the Trauma Tree?"

Charles pulled himself up from the branch, and with a very shaky voice said, "As you all are well aware, of the two broods of youngsters both my late wife Clemmie and myself reared this year, there is only my boy Chico and Char left out of the whole twelve eggs. They were born as good healthy youngsters, but for some reason, fate has dealt us some shocking blows. We all remember the night of the bad storm, when our nest was waterlogged and only one survived—Chico. The hard thing about this was that they all had been practising with their flight feathers the night before, and were preparing for the big one next day. You all know about Clemmie and the second nest when Char was the only one to escape when Mauler and Marsha Magpie found the nest and ripped it apart with their beaks. Char dropped straight through the bottom of the nest, then landed on the ground, pretending to be dead by keeping still until I found her and took her to my sister's growing family at Bluebell Way. She's only been back with us at No 79 for four weeks and has got involved with the other culprits during that time. Yes, you have my total agreement, for she must respect what we've all tried to do for her since she was preserved to fight another day."

You could hear the sighs of relief when Charles Chaffinch made that final statement, for there was no doubt in anyone's mind that lack of proper parentage seemed to be the main reason for youngsters to go off the rails. Ninety-nine per cent of the parents all looked uncomfortable, knowing that each was guilty of this offence.

Grandpa Jim now realising that all the major items on his agenda had been carefully discussed, noticed a movement in the bottom left-hand side of the perched parents and, sure enough, it was Char who had made her way up through the lower branches and was now, it appeared, ready to receive some instruction, for she looked directly at Grandpa Jim and said, "Dear Pops, and Grandpa Jim, I am quite

prepared to go along with everyone's suggestion that I go with Spick, Span and Sparkle Blackbird, Steph and Sophie Starling, Bobbie Blue-tit and Trudie Great Tit." And then, typical of this head-strong winged flapper, she declared, "Whatever happens in the Trauma Tree will not make any difference to how I behave after I've served my Bird time!"

Grandpa Jim looked sternly at her and said, "Shall we wait and see? Please remember that union is strength and, while you are all together, you must use this to keep you all in good spirits. I don't want any forbidden items brought under your wings and you all will be thoroughly vetted by Midge and Millie Mistle Thrush. Then you will follow me to take up your temporary lodgings."

Finally he said, "I can assure you all that the Smart Sparrow has had almost identical situations through many years and many generations. There has never been an occasion when this punishment was not successful. In fact, when the neighbourhood had twenty times as many birds of all species as there are flying about today, you can understand why The Smart Sparrow had such a difficult time in organising and arranging safe passages through hostile shrub, tree, or cover, backwards and forwards to the Trauma Tree. And he always had to make sure the predator birds had been well informed by Digger the Crow. And I can assure you all that Digger is still doing a grand job for us and is already, on my instruction, arranging for safe passages for tomorrow. Now have you anything left in your half-orange saucer? If so let's drink a toast to the Smart Sparrow and may the next time we meet be proof that this will all have been worthwhile and a rewarding conclusion is the outcome."

He declared the meeting over, with all parents under strict instructions to bring the offenders to No 63's clothes line, the roundabout one, when the church clock struck three. Grandpa Jim took Stan Starling to one side and told him that as he had not visited the Trauma Tree for some time, he would have to go over in the morning and clear the branches, which were the usual ones used for the perch punishment platforms. Looking at his own now empty coconut, he said to himself, "I am glad I am not travelling too far. I think I have had enough medicine for today. What a day!"

Grandpa Jim also told Stan Starling that Jaws the Jackdaw has let him know that a few dozen starlings were passing through and were boarding in local trees for several nights while they awaited more company from up north, so he wanted him to arrange with their leader to park up in the top of the Trauma Tree, perhaps for tomorrow night, just for a couple of hours and see how things worked out. Stan gave a loud chuckle at this for he knew how much Grantley the Starling Sovereign enjoyed these little engagements. There were no rewards for anyone concerned, except the pleasure it gave everyone to help those regions who were trying to keep their community free from modern-day thinking. So often the older birds worked hard but found that red tape blighted the progressive outlook that most of the Councillors tried to adopt. He said to Grandpa Jim, "I have no doubt but that he will be in charge himself."

At the first strike of the church clock at eight a.m. Grandpa Jim made his way to the Trauma Tree, and, sure thing, just as he suspected, the whole of the tree's branches and twigs had made a massive amount of growth, shooting out thorns, so that the branch which had always been used, and which the eight detainees would perch on, was barely recognisable. It was really going to test his beak and claws. He set to work with real gusto, working along the top of the bough, removing every thorn from its base, and then working underneath by gripping the top part of the bough with one set of claws and tearing out with beak and claws the lower parts, working along upside down until he had cleared approximately eight feet of wood, leaving a hole with the diameter being roughly ten inches. As he expected, when he hopped along the branch to review his work from where he had started, a thin trickle of sap was oozing from each torn-out thorn root. He tried some, for his handiwork had taken a fair amount of energy from his frail little body. He gave an immense sigh of satisfaction for this was heavenly nectar.

He recalled how, in the driest summer on record many, many years ago, the Smart Sparrow had used the Trauma Tree with its magical liquids to supply nearly all the neighbourhood's small bird residents. They had come along to quench their thirst, and in those days the Butcher Bird, (red-backed shrike) used part of this tree for his spoils. There was hardly any water anywhere, for the three wells nearby had been declared dry and the Smart Sparrow had devised another method for getting the lifeblood of the FFS to their parched throats but, as Grandpa Jim reminded himself, there would be another time to tell that story.

He soon realised that any one of the eight doing bird time would soon be thinking, that with all this luxury available to them, eating and drinking this nectar, it was on a par with having digs in the Long Legs' Queen's Palace. Then he remembered there was going to be a surprise or two in store for the Borough's Bird Brain Brawlers. Little did he know that maybe there would be a few more as well, from an unexpected quarter and one of those was going to occur very shortly—which might cause a few anxious moments.

Even where he was perched on this branch meditating, pondering the consequences of the starlings' proposed visit, he found he was automatically popping out his beak, and letting the aphids just drop straight onto his tongue. How delicious! He had not taken a lot of notice of this immediate food source, but they was every colour imaginable, green, black, grey, even red and purple, and very moorish. Then, glancing upwards, both his beady eyes followed the trunk of the Trauma Tree; it was about eight feet high at this point, towards the formation of the T-piece, a good twelve feet above this, so from the ground it would have to be about twenty feet, from where the branches tapered out in tree-shape directions. One advantage, though,

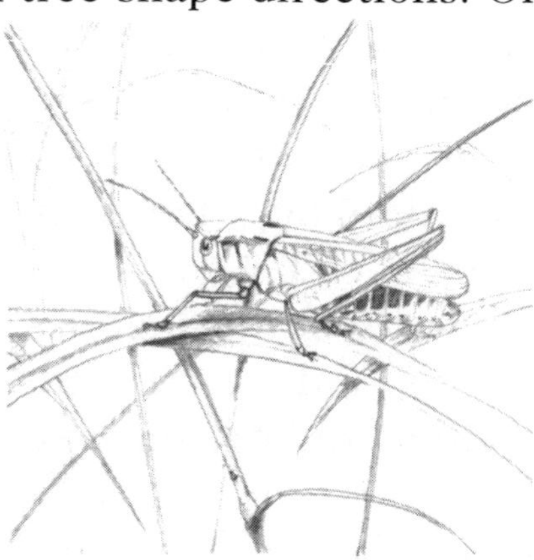

everywhere you looked there was no let-up with the thorns. Deciding to make a quick flight up and down through the Trauma Tree, he discovered there was nothing like as many aphids in the upper branches as in the lower two-thirds and he also noticed the thorns had a needle-sharp tip. He even felt a slight ache as he perched on a cluster of them. His feet and claws had reinforced skin, another of his inherited awards, so this was just what the doctor ordered, and this part of the Trauma Tree would certainly be serving its purpose for the Brain Brawlers.

Whilst taking in the whole of the tree from this lofty position, he again considered that something would have to be done about this splendid food provision, for this was not going to be any sort of punishment. Somehow he would have to find ways and means to remove most, if not all of these aphids, before he collected the eight offenders at three p.m.

Hopping back down and once more perched on the branch he had cleared and hearing a sound down below, he called out, "Who's there?"

A squeaky voice replied, "It's only me, Grandpa Jim." He knew this could only be Fairface the Fox (so named for as a young cub she'd had very pale fur, and even now was quite distinctive), as she was a good pal to nearly everyone, and always doing errands for either two- or four-footers of the neighbourhood's nature community, and was good pals with some Long Legs as well.

"Just the job," Grandpa Jim said, quickly telling her the reason why he was in the Trauma Tree. "I think you might be able to help me, for as this is to be a form of punishment whilst they are in the Tree, the one thing we do not want it to be is a four-star hotel. If we can clear three-quarters of the aphids it will be wonderful, but it doesn't give us much time for the church clock has just struck twelve, and I am bringing them in at three." There followed a very quick conversation, with Grandpa Jim excitedly nodding his head in agreement to the agreed proposals, Fairface's brush waving in time with his movements.

Then, watching her disappear in the direction of the nearby cricket club where she had made friends with the Long Legs Head Groundsman, Grandpa Jim looked round to make sure that all was in order for the incoming tenants. He noticed that all the thorns had quickly healed over and were no longer oozing nectar, but, as soon as he gave a little peck to the site of the removed thorn, it started up again, much to his delight.

The more he stopped here, remembering and recollecting the various incidents that had occurred in the Trauma Tree, the more vivid his memory became, especially when he heard a flap of large wings and, looking up, saw it was Diva, Digger the Crow's wife. She was the same as Digger, a very friendly crow and was even worse than Digger when it came to passing on bits of news—always lengthened by her embellishments. What was she doing here, he wondered?

She called down to Grandpa Jim, "What's this I hear about the Trauma Tree been used for the small bird offenders? It's a great idea, for they're already been called pests by all of us larger wings. When are they moving in to receive their punishment stay? I did hear there was twenty of all species. Scud and Speedy were telling me and Digger that it's next week some time."

Well it's not very often that Grandpa Jim told any porkies, but in this instance he considered that it would be wise not to divulge that time of entry was within the next few hours, for though the young culprits were going to be well looked after with regard to their safety whilst in the Trauma Tree, there was always the risk of rogue predators—large wings who would try to snaffle a tasty meal. So Grandpa Jim replied, "It's not been decided yet. Anyhow, who told you that piece of news?"

Diva replied, "Digger was busy in the cricket field and overheard those starlings from up north saying their special strike force was standing by to deliver some material matter before they moved on, I don't know what that might be, but there is another six weeks to go before Christmas—though quite often Xmas does come early for some birds, I do agree. Is there any news you wanted to let our cousins Ronnie and Rene Rook have for they are visiting the new ploughed fields of Long Legs Farmer Monkham and I am just going over to see them?" And with a great big spread of wings she took off, not much wiser for her visit.

Grandpa Jim had hardly said a word and wondered why. Not only was the Long Legs world made up of people who had missed out on something, but also the bird world. Like he had said many times, not only inwardly to himself, but outwardly as well, it takes all sorts. One thing he could be sure of, Diva was a jolly good mum, and made sure that no harm was ever done to their youngsters, and she always had a spick and span nest. There was a sad story he remembered, concerning the three tall lime trees at the other side of the Green. A relative of Digger had provided and maintained the nest on the very topmost forked branch of one, and brought up in several successive years lots of youngsters. One year his wife was run over by a Long Legs motor car and he had been away searching for food, so didn't know what had happened. He brought up the family and for the next couple of years each spring he would methodically clear, tidy up and rebuild the nest in preparation for her return, which never happened.

Grandpa Jim, hearing the clock strike one o'clock, said, "I must be on my way, back to headquarters."

He decided that he must get cracking for not only had he to make sure that everyone was able to pass the medical, but he also had to complete the arrangements for some other entertainment he wanted to arrange, but he was quietly confident he would get the OK for that. It might well be that, as the Borough's Long Legs had kept this a well-kept secret, the surprise might be a lot noisier than he dared to imagine.

What a bit of luck! He had reached the end of the Green when he noticed that Jaws the Jackdaw was scrounging around in the rubbish, which was waiting to be collected by the Long Legs Bin Men. Jaws knew that he would often find all sorts of valuables. He stopped and had a few words with the jackdaw, assuring him that if he did Grandpa

Jim this particular favour he would be well rewarded. His final words were, "Make sure they are made secure, and there must be eight pieces."

There was nothing delighted Jaws more than being given a task that could improve his reputation around the neighbourhood, for he was always being accused of taking things when others were to blame. Only last week Long Legs had pointed at him flying past, and had shook a finger at him, shouting, "Bring that ring back, it's been in the family for many years!" At the time Jaws knew who had taken it, though it was more than he dared to report the culprit, though most of the FFS knew who it was.

Grandpa Jim arrived back at the Dez Rez to find that Midge the Medic Mistle had been round to check each one of the eight. One remained unchecked, and Midge told Grandpa Jim, "Char seems to have disappeared again but I do know she is all right, for Charles only brought her in to the Medical Centre last week and she was in excellent shape then, considering what she had been through."

Grandpa Jim had made himself look respectable with an extra shine to his pristine chest feathers, using some polish that Jaws had found and kept under one of his wings. As Jaws told Grandpa Jim, "It only comes out on special occasions." It was now time to leave for No 63. On his arrival he was surprised to find that nearly every small bird from the various properties had collected from their respective gardens. There must be at least thirty different pairs of birds, and all had gathered on the clothes-line roundabout, awaiting their leader. Each parent felt quietly humbled as he told them that this episode in their lives was not only for their benefit, but also for the neighbourhood's. Looking round, he noticed that Char was present and was sitting next to Tillie Great Tit. He asked her, "Do you think you deserve to go to the Trauma Tree, Char?—for as you are aware, your name comes up repeatedly, for getting involved with your other pals, and causing concern amongst us all. You don't seem to realise this gives us all a bad name in the FFS and the Long Legs Society. Even Four-Footed Friends were concerned."

She replied in a clear, calm voice. "You can do what you like, I am not going to change."

Then came a scare for everyone, perched up and awaiting Grandpa Jim's final briefing. Jaws the Jackdaw arrived and landed on the centre pole: "There is smoke coming from the Trauma Tree, it's going straight up from the centre of it," he announced.

Grandpa Jim replied, "Super, that's the first part of our step into humility, we'll call that Stage One.

Nothing to worry about. Now, before we all move off, I want to tell you about the bird that mislaid the rules of flying along the path, which most of the parents here usually try to follow, it goes like this."

Then very slowly, making sure that each line was taken in by the culprits, who were all perched next to each other, he commenced.

It's easy to judge if you have the health,
And Bird heaven makes you rule for a day,
Fly to a mirror and look at yourself,
And see what that bird has to say.

It's not your dad, mum, sister, brother, or wife,
An opinion on you must pass,
The bird whose decisions score most in your life,
Is the bird looking back from the glass.

Birds of all sizes confirm that you're cool,
Others say nothing but sigh,
The bird in the glass says you are a fool,
If you can't look him straight in the eye.

The bird in the glass—disregard the rest—
Is the bird right through to the end,
setting examples and never a pest
for the bird in the glass is your friend.

Perhaps you fool your pals along the flights of life,
Maybe you receive 'well done' as you pass,
The lasting reward will be heartache and tears,
If you've deceived the bird in the glass.

"It's of no importance where we are, but the flight path that we travel on must be the right and only way."

As usual he flapped his wings to say he had finished. "Now let's go to Stage Two," he concluded. Everyone gathered were still spellbound with Grandpa Jim's little summary, each still looking at one another and looking round at other parents who were just as affected. Grandpa Jim left them and with a flap of his wings, said to the eight offenders, "Right, follow me." The flight across, as the bird flies, was direct, passing over Albert the Cricket Club Groundsman who was just leaving the Green with a container.

Looking down on Albert, Grandpa Jim acknowledged him with a loop-the-loop action, and was still in front of the pack of eight. Seeing this, and looking upwards, Albert waved his container from side to side, and clearly he was delighted with what he had done to help the FFS.

By this time their flight had taken them to the base of the Tree, where they all landed on the raised earth and listened to Grandpa Jim. Clearly, they were quite distressed, for the smell of tar hang heavily in the air. But he said, "Now, the

smell is nothing to worry about, for Albert has disinfected the aphids which were infesting the Trauma Tree. Not one has come to any harm, they have just cleared off. Now, I want you all to hop up onto the branch you see above you."

Char had already spotted the eight pieces of what she thought looked like glass hanging down in front of the branch. They were, indeed, pieces of mirror. "Grandpa Jim, what's the idea of the looking glass?" Her words were hardly out of her beak, where she was now perched on the branch surveying herself in one of the mirrors. Then Sparkle, one of the blackbird youngsters noticed the earth moving down below, and straightaway dived down to devour a nice juicy grub. (A mole was practising.)

Grandpa Jim, now perched up above them all, on a bough with clusters of thorns all round said, "Come back up here, Sparkle, for this is not what you are in the Trauma Tree for! You have to decide, amongst yourselves, which four go down, and you'll have to be satisfied with what the moles are providing. And when the moles pack up working, after about twenty minutes, so the other four will have to wait until it's your turn. When I explained this to you all in the meeting room, you should have been listening! As I'm sure you heard, the clock on the Green has just struck four o'clock, so, before I take up my position, higher up the tree, are you all clear that you have to stop here for forty-eight hours? You will find also that there is no need to be thirsty, for if you tap the bark where a thorn has been removed, you will find this liquid will satisfy your taste buds. There are now no-go areas all around the Trauma Tree. There might well be some more visitors; some of them you might say will be welcome ones, some you might say they are not. Remember you have seven others for company," and with that he flew high up in the top branches.

He had lost count of the stages he had considered earlier, but all was going smoothly. Up here he looked about, and reminded himself how things were working out so far.

At this height there was still a hint of a smell from the tar, and there were also a few aphids hanging about (the odd ones dropping down) but the bulk of them had disappeared completely. Albert had done a good job. Jaws had made a splendid effort with the mirrors, hanging them at just the right distance and height, so even if they wanted to (and he was sure they would) they were just too far out of reach to be removed. Jaws had also wiped something round the rims, which appeared to be a gluey substance—not harmful, but nastily unpleasant to touch and smell. Muffler the King Mole had kept his word, and had sent two instead of four Molers. It wouldn't make a lot of difference, because they would still only be guided by their own tummies, the usually regulated four hours between their meals. Grandpa Jim wondered if it had anything to do with the clock on the church on the Green, for they had hearing second to none. Then he considered again; sometimes their tunnels were two feet under the surface and he doubted very much if they could hear the clock striking its peals all that way down. He had not thought much about how deep the Molers would be working; he would have to get a message to them via Fairface the Friendly Fox not to burrow too deep for the youngsters doing bird time when they needed meals.

All was quiet down below (no doubt they were preening themselves in their very own mirrors), and he was sure that the more they looked at their reflections in the mirrors, the more they would surely be thinking what kind of birds were they to get themselves in to such a pickle, perched up in the Trauma Tree all night. They had a long time in which to do some careful thinking! He flew quietly away.

He arrived back at the Des Res, just in time to see Fairface the Friendly Fox going home to her lair, which fortunately was in the direction of the Green. Grandpa Jim landed just above her and passed the message on about the depths he thought the Molers should be working at, if they were to provide food for the culprits. "No problem, that's fine," she replied. "By the way, I have heard that Long Legs are arriving about eight o'clock but they are only stopping for ten minutes," and with that she sloped off.

Grandpa Jim had an uneasy night, for he wondered how the fireworks (this was one of the surprises) had affected the youngsters, especially Char Chaffinch, given her rebellious remark: “I am not going to change.” What he’d heard a couple of hundred metres away was only the swish of the fireworks as they were lit. They’d illuminated the whole dark night, for the moon had decided to hide behind clouds.

‘Experimental Purposes’, that was what the sparrow grapevine heard. He heard the clock on the Green strike six. Just as dawn was breaking, a message had come to him on his Registration Bough that the starling boys had moved in quite early, starting and completing their task and were already grouping to move on. Grantley the Sovereign Starling had also told Grandpa Jim that any time he wanted their help, he would be only too pleased to be of assistance.

Oh dear, oh dear, what have they done! Grandpa Jim immediately dropped everything, and flew straight to the Trauma Tree and was met by Char sitting on the earth mound totally covered in starling pooh and surrounded by the other seven delinquents equally afflicted. She said, “Speaking for all of us, Grandpa Jim, we all promise not to misbehave any more.” She told him what had gone on through the night—the Owl swishing round so often, the fireworks, which had alarmed them all, and the starlings overhead. Surely now that they would all show remorse for their behaviour?

“Don’t you think that we all have been punished

enough, just look at the state we are all in?" she continued. "How on earth do you think we shall be able to fly back into our bird haunts looking like this?" Grandpa Jim had weighed up the situation as soon as he arrived, thinking to himself what a super job the starling boys had done, and, looking up, discovered that the branch they had decided to launch their drop from was just a little off centre from the Trauma Tree's trunk. Anything dropping vertically would make a direct hit on anything below, so this was without doubt a splendid strategy and expert control. Jaws the Jackdaw must have had been involved, he instantly thought, and he was proved correct, before the day was through.

The situation needed careful thinking over, for no way could the youngsters fly back, even to the Dez Rez, for the starling pooh was highly offensive and strong-smelling. As he could clearly see, the white-blue gluey droppings were clinging and attaching to every part of their shivering little bodies. They could never get lift-off, because they were weighed down with the noxious matter.

A flutter of wings and Stan Starling came flying in, landed beside Grandpa Jim. Quickly looking round, he had difficulty in identifying his three nieces, Steph, Shelia, and Sophie. It was only because they were sitting next to each other and had made an effort to draw his attention to themselves that he realised that they were indeed his nieces. Like the rest of this sad bedraggled bunch, they looked mighty sorry for themselves and were almost totally unrecognisable.

Grandpa Jim asked, “How did you get across the no-go areas, Stan? With my pass, I’m able to fly into the Trauma Tree from the church side without any worries.”

Stan Starling answered, “I came through the kindness of Fairface the Friendly Fox, who gave me a ride on her back. She says did you want her to run any errands for you, Grandpa Jim? She is round the other side of the Trauma Tree waiting if you want a message taken to Albert the Groundsman.” This was an astonishing bit of luck, for Grandpa Jim had wondered how he was going to get a message across to Albert. He was the only one who could provide the cleansing materials that were needed to make all the now very sad and remorseful youngsters clean and respectable again.

Flying round to Fairface the Friendly Fox, Grandpa Jim settled on the branch above her and told her what he needed. He also asked her to let Albert know that this favour would be returned in full for he would organise, through the FFS over the next few months, a good beak-digging of the outfield round the Cricket Square to aerate it.

Would Albert come as quickly as possible, before he started work for the day? As Grandpa Jim was saying this, the clock on the church struck seven o'clock.

What on earth were the parents of those poor youngsters going to say if any one of them managed to get across the Green and saw them in this foul-smelling state—covered in putrid, slimy, sludgy, rancid, clingy, congealing bird droppings? It seemed ages before any of them could utter any sensible words, for Grandpa Jim was finding it difficult to recall any event of this magnitude happening at any time during his long life, through so many generations. Well, there had been the time when Farmer Monkham had upset some large churns which contained several gallons of Mrs Monkham's freshly made parsnip wine in the farmyard. The liquid had formed a tiny lake and after they had all consumed a large quantity, himself included, they had been knocked for six! Yes, he had been one of the many sparrows who had whetted their temptations. What a story!

"You there, Grandpa Jim," Albert called out, "I'll leave the bucket and trays just outside. When you are done with them, tell Fairface the Friendly Fox, and I'll pick them up later." Grandpa Jim addressed each of the now wide-awake well humbled young birds: "I want you to try to move your wings; if you can't, just hop across to where Albert has left the bucket with the cleansing liquid—will you all be able to manage that?" Each one nodded their agreement as they waddled slowly across. Albert had left both bucket and trays just under the spread of the Trauma Tree so they were concealed from prying flying eyes, but so close to the covering branches that Grandpa Jim had to wrench out a few nasty, protruding sharp thorns that were going to cause problems when the young birds started their ablutions.

This was just what he wanted, the bucket with the tap near the bottom. He could see how clogged up as they tried to move just this short distance. Pulling the first tray under the tap with his trusty bill, he turned on the tap, filled it to a manageable height and with both claws and beak, moved it nearer, so each bird had freedom to do what birds do best, make a big splash. The first one, as you can guess was Char and as soon as she hopped into the tray, she chirruped with delight, for Albert had put some of his fragrant aftershave in the bucket, to give it a nice aroma.

Grandpa Jim was glad that Stan Starling was looking after his nieces for they were finding it difficult to see, with the gooey material beginning to close up their vision. As soon as each bird had its own tray, they began to enjoy this communal bathing, each of them noticing the other birds' identities gradually returning. In fact after several minutes they were all remarking to each other,

"You're even cleaner than when you came in yesterday!' Both Stan Starling and Grandpa Jim watched this transformation unfold, and, as you can gather, it gave them both an enormous amount of pleasure.

Each of them had come to the same conclusion, that now they were quite tidy and presentable, they all should be granted their freedom. Grandpa Jim, having the last word on any decision taken and not needing the rest of the committee's approval said to Stan Starling, "Do you think any of the young birds will be showing any remorse or regret for what they were involved in—that led to this trip to the Trauma Tree?"

His words were hardly out of his bill, when Char flew up and perched on the same bough, which had somehow been cleaned of all the noxious starling pooh droppings, and said, "Grandpa Jim, we have all been talking about what we have done in the past. Each one of us promises that we will not misbehave again, nor cause our own families untold worries, nor make all the neighbourhood dislike us. We all agree that never again will we do anything that might upset you all. Please could you let us all have our freedom now?"

Stan and Grandpa

Jim were instantly taken aback by this very humble chaffinch chatter, and for an instant Grandpa Jim appeared lost for words—after all, of all the youngsters who had raised hell, and given Char's reaction to the proposed Trauma Tree punishment before they came over, he had considered her to be one coarse, churlish, chaffinch, who was not going to respond to any criticism, chastisement, or correction at all.

Quickly he recovered his composure, saying to her, "Both Stan and myself speak for the rest of the Borough's FFS. It appears that you all are very repentant over your past misdemeanours. I might say that not only has this been an eye-opener for you all, but it was an experiment for us to see if it would work. Our objective was to make sure that you recognised that what you had done was very degrading, discreditable and disgraceful. The extra maltreatment from our starling friends from up north not only added an extra ingredient to our proposed shaming and humiliating of you all, but it also helped us see how we all want you to play a big role in your society—the birds of today, and future generations of all colours and creeds. Yes, of course we are going to let you have your freedom again. Now I have to make arrangements for you to fly safely back across the Green, which you all understand is still prohibited—Scud and Speedy Sparrow Hawk are still licensed to enjoy whatever is wandering through." But with his usual sense of humour, he added, "Though, smelling like you all do like a Paris perfume shop, I doubt if they would come anywhere near you!"

Looking down at the other seven happy-faced youngsters, Grandpa Jim said, "I want to hear you all say and confirm what Char Chaffinch has said: do you all agree to be upstanding birds of fine character, and make the neighbourhood a happier place to enjoy for both Long Legs and the FFS?"

With one voice they all shouted, "Yes, we do, Grandpa Jim."

Grandpa Jim, knowing it was now safe to cross the Green had a brief encounter with Jaws the Jackdaw on his way back to the Dez Rez. The jackdaw stopped to ask, "How effective was Grantley Starling's strike force, did it register any hits at all?"

Grandpa Jim replied, "I have never seen anything so accurately placed, whatever wonders did you work, Jaws?"

Jaws replied quite truthfully, "I dropped a strong thread plumbline down from the marker bough they were sitting on and was guided by the reflections from the pieces of mirrors, so it was a piece of cake, and just had to be exact."

Arriving at headquarters, Grandpa Jim just could not

believe his eyes for right across the length of the long clothes line there must have been every tiny bird in the neighbourhood—even all the Red Robins from Nos 49 to 59 who must have been eight pairs. Altogether, quickly counting, he could see at least fifty birds. And what a welcome they gave him for each pair gave him songful notes he would remember for a long time. The melodies gave him memories of past days and the Dawn Chorus he had always so enjoyed being part and parcel of.

Feathers and Fur

Characters mentioned, and their families

Grandpa Jim (Beaver Bill, the Smart Sparrow)
Spotter the Skylark
Charles Chaffinch, daughter Charlotte (Char), son Chico, his late wife Clemmie
George and Georgina Greenfinch
His twin brother Grumbler, Gill, the foster mum to Gerald and Geoff
Two of his named offspring of Five with his late wife, Gemima
Thomas and Tilly Great Tit, daughter Trudie
Stan and Samantha Starling, brother Spindle Starling, and his youngsters, Steph, Sheila, and Sophie
Grantley the Starling Sovereign
Goldie and Gladys Goldfinch
The Blackbird Boys Spick, Span and Sparkle

Scud and Speedy Sparrow Hawk
Muffler the King Mole
Wise Old Owl
Trencher The Thinking Tawny
Jaws the Jackdaw
Billy and Belle Blue Tit, daughter Bobbie
Mauler and Marsha Magpie
Midge and Millie Mistle Thrush
The Butcher Bird (Red Backed Shrike)
Fairface, the Friendly Fox
Digger and Diva Crow
Ronnie and Rene Rook
Farmer Monkham, Mrs Monkham
Albert the Long Legs Cricket Club Groundsman
Eight pairs of Red Robins

FFS: Feathered Friend Society
The Fours Bs: Borough's Bird Brain Brawlers